THE ATTACK ON THE PENTAGON ON SEPTEMBER 11, 2001

Carolyn Gard

The Rosen Publishing Group, Inc.
New York

Published in 2003 by The Rosen Publishing Group, Inc.
29 East 21st Street, New York, NY 10010

Copyright © 2003 by The Rosen Publishing Group, Inc.

First Edition

All rights reserved. No part of this book may be reproduced in any form without permission in writing from the publisher, except by a reviewer.

Library of Congress Cataloging-in-Publication Data

Gard, Carolyn.
The attack on the Pentagon on September 11, 2001/by Carolyn Gard.—1st ed.
  p. cm.—(Terrorist attacks)
Summary: Describes the events of September 11, 2001, focusing on American Airlines Flight 77, which was hijacked by terrorists and flown into the Pentagon.
Includes bibliographical references and index.
ISBN   978-1-4358-9080-0
1. Terrorism—United States—Juvenile literature. 2. September 11 Terrorist Attacks, 2001—Juvenile literature. 3. Pentagon (Va.)—Juvenile literature. 4. Qaida (Organization)—Juvenile literature. [1. Terrorism. 2. September 11 Terrorist Attacks, 2001. 3.Pentagon (Va.) 4. Qaida (Organization)]
I. Title. II. Series.
HV6432.5.Q2 G37 2003
975.5'295044—dc21

                                                                  2002009694

Manufactured in the United States of America

CONTENTS

	Introduction	4
Chapter 1	The Pentagon	7
Chapter 2	Al Qaeda	15
Chapter 3	Preparations	25
Chapter 4	The Attack	33
Chapter 5	The Cleanup and Investigation	43
Chapter 6	The Aftermath	51
	Glossary	57
	For More Information	58
	For Further Reading	60
	Bibliography	61
	Index	63

INTRODUCTION

The Pentagon is more than a building. It is the symbol of the military might of the United States. The building sits low to the ground, massive and strong. From the air it is a unique geometric figure. The Pentagon gets attention because of its size and its purpose. It was designed for efficiency, not for beauty. To some people, the Pentagon building represents the military power of the United States. Others see the structure and are reminded that wars bring death and destruction.

When terrorists hijacked a plane and flew it into the Pentagon on September 11, 2001, there was little debate about the meaning of the building. The terrorists had tried to destroy one of the United States's most important institutions. However, the terrorists failed to understand that Americans are like a family. They may disagree and even fight about many issues, but they will not tolerate an outsider's attempt to destroy their country. In the months following the harrowing events of

On September 11, 2001, hijacked airliner American Airlines Flight 77 was crashed into the west face of the Pentagon, causing extensive damage.

September 11, restoring the damaged Pentagon came to symbolize the determination of the United States to win the war against terrorism.

The rebuilt Pentagon was celebrated in a ceremony on September 11, 2002, exactly sixty-one years after the ground-breaking for the building in 1941 and one year after the attack. Before the fires from the September 11, 2001, attack were put out, Pentagon renovation manager W. Lee Evey told the workers, "Build it again, build it even better, and don't look back."

Firefighters attempt to put out flames at the Pentagon on September 11, 2001, after the crash of American Airlines Flight 77.

THE PENTAGON

CHAPTER 1

In 1939, on the eve of World War II, the United States War Department had 24,000 employees scattered in seventeen buildings in Washington, D.C., and Virginia. These facilities included just about every option—apartment houses, garages, warehouses, and residences. By 1941 the U.S. Army alone had grown from 270,000 employees to 1.4 million employees. The department no longer fit in its headquarters in the Munitions Building.

The spread-out quarters led to serious delays in both information gathering and decision making. At a time when Adolf Hitler was threatening to move

The Attack on the Pentagon on September 11, 2001

into Africa, and as the relations between the United States and Japan deteriorated, efficiency in the military become essential.

A Single Structure

Brigadier General Brehon Somervell, who had headed the construction division of the War Department, suggested that the country have a single building to house the entire War Department and its staff. His idea interested both the War Department and Congress.

For several months, the War Department had been looking for a place to build temporary structures to house its growing staff. Congress had approved the funds for this move, but with the restriction that the structures be located in the District of Columbia. Such a large site didn't exist within the city limits. There was, however, a perfect site in Virginia. Arlington Farms lay across the Potomac River from Washington. The federal government already owned the land.

The tract of land has an interesting and patriotic history. In 1778, John Parke Custis, a stepson of George Washington, bought the land. Custis's granddaughter married Robert E. Lee and brought the land into the Lee family. In 1883, the federal government bought the land from the Lee estate for $150,000.

In July 1941, Somervell discussed his idea with Representative Clifton Woodrum of Virginia. Woodrum was a member of the House Appropriations Committee and

The Pentagon

headed the subcommittee that considered construction projects. Woodrum asked Somervell for detailed drawings. Somervell wasted no time. He immediately got engineers and architects and gave them five days to come up with plans for a building. Somervell wanted the building to be fireproof, air-conditioned, able to house 40,000 people, and no more than three stories high.

The drafters worked through the weekend. To make the building as efficient as possible, they chose a pentagon shape. A five-sided building wasn't totally new; many of the country's early forts were pentagons. The design consisted of two rings with an inner courtyard. Connections between the rings made each wing look like a comb. The building would be twice the area of the Empire State Building. The cost to build it would be $35 million.

Many people objected to the design. They argued that the building was too big for the local water and sewer facilities, it cost too much, it wasn't in Washington, the location would mar the view of the city from Arlington National Cemetery, and the building would certainly not be used after the war. These objections were overruled when President Franklin D. Roosevelt gave his approval to the project. On July 28, 1941, a little over a month after Somervell started on his design, Congress granted the money to build the Pentagon.

President Roosevelt signed the bill allocating the money. However, he wanted the location changed to

Early construction on the Pentagon in 1942. The ground-breaking ceremony took place on September 11, 1941, and the building was dedicated on January 15, 1943.

preserve the view from the cemetery. Although the new site was only ten feet above the level of the river and would require more construction, Somervell agreed to the change. Roosevelt also wanted the size of the building reduced by half and to have only 20,000 employees. After the war, the building would be used to store records.

Construction Begins

Ground was broken for the Pentagon on September 11, 1941. An old airplane hangar on the site became the headquarters for the hundreds of drafters and architects who worked on the building. Because the construction was a rush job, the designing and building work went on together. In order to keep up with the building progress, the architects made new drawings every night. The machines for reproducing prints ran twenty-four hours a day. They put out 12,000 to 30,000 prints a week.

As the planning went on, some of the specifications changed. The building became five stories with five rings. Corridors connected the rings, and the spacing between them let natural light into the building. Many building materials were scarce because they were needed for the war effort. The designs used reinforced concrete instead of steel for the walls. This saved 38,000 tons of steel, enough steel to build a battleship. The materials for the concrete came from the Potomac River itself. Barges brought the sand and gravel from the river to the building site. There they were fed into trucks and mixed on the way to the construction site. The use of ramps instead of passenger elevators saved more steel. The

FACTS AND FIGURES ABOUT THE PENTAGON

Total land area	583 acres
Building area	29 acres
Area of center courtyard	5 acres
Construction workers	13,000
Parking capacity	9,500 vehicles
Floor area	6,500,000 sq. ft.
Stairways	150
Escalators	19
Freight elevators	13
Rest rooms	280
Windows	7,748
Lamp replacements (daily)	250
Employees (2002)	23,000

Amenities: power plant, police force, fire station, child-care center, mini-mall, cafeterias

A 1945 aerial photograph of the Pentagon shows the roads and cloverleaf intersections surrounding it.

only substitution that proved to be unwise was the use of asbestos in ducts to save steel. Years later the disease-causing asbestos had to be removed.

The five-sided ring design fit the criteria of efficiency. The farthest a person might have to walk from one part of the building to another is 1,800 feet, about a third of a mile. Even walking slowly, a person could do this in less than ten minutes.

At the time the Pentagon was built, segregation of blacks and whites was common, especially in the South. Although separate rest rooms and lunchrooms were built for blacks and whites in the Pentagon, the "Whites" and "Coloreds" signs were never put up.

When the Japanese attacked Pearl Harbor in December 1941, the pace of construction at the Pentagon increased. In April 1942, less than eight months after the ground-breaking, 300 employees moved into the first completed section. The Pentagon was officially completed on January 15, 1943. About 33,000 people worked in the building.

Pentagon Remains Necessary

After World War II, the United States still needed a large military presence to deal with the unstable world during the Cold War years (1945–1991). Any thoughts that the Pentagon would no longer be needed were quickly forgotten. As the needs of the military grew, changes were made to the Pentagon. Open spaces were closed off to make offices. Due to security reasons and because noxious fumes seeped into the building, the bus and taxi tunnels in the building were made into offices.

As the symbol of war and the United States military, the Pentagon has been the object of demonstrations. One of the biggest occurred in 1967 when 25,000 to 30,000 people showed up to protest the United States's involvement in the Vietnam War.

In light of the September 11 attacks, two historical comments about the Pentagon proved to be prophetic. In 1941, Gilmore Clarke, the head of the Washington, D.C., Commission on Fine Arts, said, "The Pentagon presented the largest target in the world for enemy bombs." In 1968, Ada Louise Huxtable, the architecture critic of the *New York Times*, wrote, "The best thing about the building . . . is that it is horizontal, not vertical: City planners, corporate clients, and architects still might ponder the usefulness of that lesson."

An Afghan anti-Taliban soldier (with rifle) escorts captured Al Qaeda members in Tora Bora on December 17, 2001.

AL QAEDA

CHAPTER 2

In the Middle East, a growing number of extremist militants flocked to a wealthy Saudi named Osama bin Laden. Bin Laden inherited $80 million when his father died. He moved to Pakistan, where he supported the Muslims in neighboring Afghanistan who were fighting against the Soviets. In the late 1980s, bin Laden set up an organization called Al Qaeda, meaning "the Base." Al Qaeda supported oppressed Muslims both militarily and financially. Al Qaeda also encouraged militant Muslims to fight non-Islamic governments with force and violence.

Osama bin Laden, Saudi fundamentalist and founder of Al Qaeda

After the war in Afghanistan, bin Laden returned to Saudi Arabia. He hated the United States because he believed that it stood for degradation and anti-Muslim ideas. He argued that the United States was not governed in a way that fit his extremist Islamic views.

Bin Laden believed that the United States supported infidel countries and organizations. These included Saudi Arabia, Egypt, Israel, and the United Nations. He resented the involvement of the United States in the 1990–1991 Persian Gulf War and in Operation Restore Hope in Somalia in 1992 and 1993. Bin Laden felt snubbed when the Saudi Arabian government turned down his proposal to remove American forces from the Arabian Peninsula and to let bin Laden and his army protect the country.

The Spread of Al Qaeda

Osama bin Laden used Al Qaeda to make the Middle East a Muslim stronghold and to spread terrorism around the world.

The headquarters of Al Qaeda remained in Afghanistan and Pakistan until 1991, when bin Laden was expelled from Saudi Arabia and moved to Sudan.

Meanwhile, Pakistani officials were upset with bin Laden's followers, who were living in tents on the Pakistan-Afghanistan border. Their militant views caused trouble. Bin Laden flew about 500 of these veterans of the Afghan War to Sudan.

Announcement of Jihad, a book written by Osama bin Laden, was found along with terrorist training manuals at an Al Qaeda training camp near Kandahar, Afghanistan.

Many of these Al Qaeda members weren't happy. There was no jihad (religious crusade) to fight in Sudan. According to Simon Reeve's book on terrorism, *The New Jackals*, Mamdouh Mahmud Salim was an associate of bin Laden's and was arrested by the German police in September of 1998. Salim told his interrogators that there were three types of men in Al Qaeda: "People who had no success in life, had nothing in their heads, and wanted to join just to keep from falling on their noses . . . people who loved their religion but had no idea what their religion meant," and people with "nothing in their heads but to fight and solve all the problems of the world with battles."

The Attack on the Pentagon on September 11, 2001

Bin Laden set up businesses in Sudan through which Al Qaeda's work could be done without attracting attention. These businesses were involved in investments, agriculture, construction, and transportation. The companies earned money for the group. They also provided a cover for the purchase and transfer of explosives, weapons, and chemicals. By pretending they were on company business, Al Qaeda officials could travel outside Sudan to plan terrorist attacks.

Osama bin Laden and Al Qaeda sponsored training camps for terrorists. Bin Laden's wealth purchased arms for these trainees. One shipment of firearms is supposed to have cost $15 million. In the camps, the fighters learned to use firearms, explosives, chemical weapons, and other weapons of mass destruction. The camps also planned attacks on U.S. targets. They conducted experiments in the use of chemical and biological weapons.

Next, bin Laden turned his attention to the development of the international aspect of Al Qaeda. He opened an office of the Advice and Reformation Committee in London. The committee worked to make Saudi Arabia conform to strict Islamic law. Bin Laden established ties with Yemen and Albania. Both of these countries had militant and oppressed Muslims. Bin Laden bought businesses in both countries and encouraged militancy among the Muslims.

After the February 1993 bombing of the World Trade Center, Federal Bureau of Investigation (FBI) agents found

Women under Taliban rule in Afghanistan were required to wear burquas, garments that covered their entire bodies, whenever they left their homes. Women who refused to follow Taliban rules could be harassed, beaten, imprisoned, or even executed.

connections between the bombers and Osama bin Laden. From then on, the Central Intelligence Agency (CIA) kept close track of his activities. In January 1996, the CIA set up a special bin Laden task force. More than eleven agencies tracked his movements. This become the most expensive investigation into a single terrorist. In 1996 pressure from the United States, Egypt, and Saudi Arabia forced Sudan to expel bin Laden. He went to Afghanistan, where he got support from Pakistan and from Mullah Mohammed Omar, the leader of the Taliban.

The Taliban, the group that ruled Afghanistan on September 11, 2001, is a group of extremist, fundamentalist Muslims who took control of the country in 1996 and set up a government with harsh laws. Many of these laws put strict restrictions on women by making them cover their entire bodies when they went outside and preventing them from getting an education or working.

The Attack on the Pentagon on September 11, 2001

Structure

Al Qaeda is an umbrella organization that connects several terrorist organizations operating in many countries. These include the Egyptian Islamic Jihad, the Islamic Group, and jihad groups in several other countries. The groundwork is done through cells. Each cell is a group of about ten to twelve men. Cells operate in at least sixty countries. The FBI has evidence of four or five Al Qaeda cells in the United States. All the group members entered the United States legally. So far authorities have not found any evidence of illegal activities by cell members.

The cells are financed by the drug trade, by taking money from Islamic charities (either legitimate ones or ones set up to funnel money to Al Qaeda), and through criminal activities. Much of bin Laden's fortune is gone, but the cells he set up are almost self-sufficient. The members work for a reward from the Islamic god, Allah, not for financial gain.

A secret society like Al Qaeda depends on trust. The nineteen hijackers of the four airplanes used in the September 11 attacks completed terrorist training in Afghanistan. Many were school friends, some had lived together for years, and others were related by family ties. These ties, which outsiders could not see, kept the terrorist network together.

Cell members are highly disciplined and patient. After September 11, neighbors of some of the hijackers remembered that the men kept to themselves and always traveled together.

Al Qaeda

COUNTRIES IN WHICH AL QAEDA HAS OPERATED

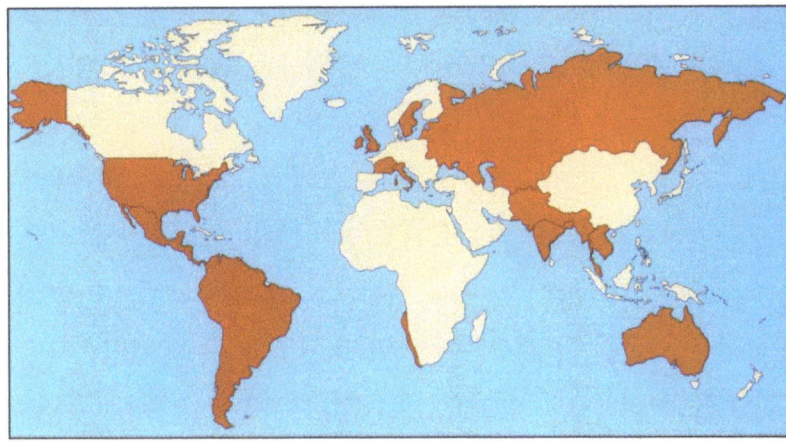

Afghanistan			
Albania			
Algeria			
Australia			
Austria			
Azerbaijan			
Bahrain			
Bangladesh			
Belgium			
Bosnia			
Egypt			
Eritrea			
France	Lebanon	Saudi Arabia	Uganda
Germany	Libya	Somalia	United Arab
India	Malaysia	South Africa	Emirates
Iran	Mauritania	Sudan	United Kingdom
Ireland	Netherlands	Switzerland	United States
Italy	Pakistan	Tajikistan	Uzbekistan
Jordan	Philippines	Tanzania	Yemen
Kenya	Qatar	Tunisia	
Kosovo	Russia	Turkey	

From the U. S. Department of State, Office of International Information Programs

When authorities retraced the steps of the hijackers, they found that some of them had waited five years for their deadly missions. Estimates of the number of Al Qaeda members worldwide range from several hundred to several thousand.

Al Qaeda has two levels of government. One level encourages militants to attack secular, or non-religious, governments. The other level of Al Qaeda is run by a council

The Attack on the Pentagon on September 11, 2001

that approves major projects. Another committee approves military projects. Evidence collected by intelligence agencies suggests that this second level carried out the attacks against the United States Embassies in Africa, the attack on the USS *Cole*, and the September 11 attacks.

Al Qaeda has not always been successful. Authorities have stopped attempts by Al Qaeda members to assassinate Pope John Paul II in Manila, Philippines, in 1994; to bomb the capitals of the United States, Israel, and several Asian countries in 1994; to destroy several transpacific flights in 1995; and to kill President Bill Clinton during a visit to the Philippines in 1995.

In 1998, the United States launched Tomahawk cruise missiles against bin Laden's Afghan headquarters. The attack did not result in the capture of bin Laden and may have brought more militants into Al Qaeda's fold. By late 1998, over twenty militant groups were part of Al Qaeda.

Before September 11, 2001, the United States had gained some information about Al Qaeda. A former member of the network revealed that Al Qaeda was trying to get nuclear and chemical weapons. Witnesses in other terrorism-related trials said that bin Laden had declared a *fatwa*, or decree, against the United States. The fatwa said that it was the duty of all Muslims to kill Americans, both military and civilian, wherever they might be found.

Al Qaeda represents a new breed of terrorist. These people are loyal to a religious ideal rather than to a state.

An aerial photo of the Zhawar Kili Support Complex in Afghanistan, which the United States attacked on August 19, 1998, after Al Qaeda bombed two U.S. Embassies in East Africa

They are willing to die for their goals. They have learned how to move around in foreign countries without attracting attention. Above all, they have a deep hatred for Americans. They want to destroy the fundamental values of the society so that the American people become weak. They justify the killing of civilians by saying that if any of the dead are innocent they will go to paradise in the afterlife.

Around 1996, several men of Middle Eastern descent entered the United States. They lived quietly in suburbs, keeping to themselves but not arousing the suspicions of their neighbors. All too soon they would become known to every American.

The CRM Airline Training Center in Scottsdale, Arizona, where hijacker Hani Hanjour received pilot training in 1996 and 1997

PREPARATIONS

CHAPTER

From 1996 to 2001, five men of Middle Eastern background and with possible ties to Al Qaeda came to the United States. During this time they lived quietly in modest apartments.

In the spring of 1996, Hani Hanjour, a twenty-five-year-old Saudi, arrived in Hollywood, Florida. He lived with a couple who were friends of his brother. He told them he wanted to get into a flight school, but he wasn't accepted to any. In May, he moved to Oakland, California.

In September 1996, Hanjour went to Scottsdale, Arizona, a suburb of Phoenix. He

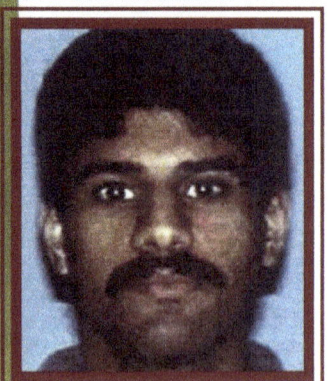

The five hijackers of American Airlines Flight 77 *(clockwise from top left)*: Hani Hanjour, Majed Moqed, Salem Alhazmi, Nawaf Alhazmi, and Khalid Almihdhar

took flight lessons at the CRM Flight School for three months. The lessons cost $4,749. In December 1997, he went back for more lessons. Hanjour wanted a private pilot's license. His flight instructor said he was a poor pilot who didn't do his homework and missed lessons. He may have gotten a commercial pilot's license for single-engine planes in Saudi Arabia in 1999.

In 1999, Hanjour moved to the United Arab Emirates. He soon returned to the United States and lived in an apartment in San Diego.

The Al Qaeda Connection

Meanwhile, in January 2000, another Saudi, Nawaf Alhazmi, twenty-four, and a Yemenite, Khalid Almihdhar, twenty-five, went to Malaysia. Secret police in Kuala

Preparations

Lumpur filmed Alhazmi and Almihdhar while the two men talked with a senior aide to Osama bin Laden. This aide was a suspect in the bombing of the USS *Cole*. The men met with other Al Qaeda members in a condominium at a resort. Alhazmi and Almihdhar told the others that they were to "kill Americans and destroy American interests and those who support America."

NETWORKING CONNECTIONS

Several social scientists have made maps showing how the hijackers were connected with one another. One of the most interesting findings of these maps is how little connection there was among the hijackers.

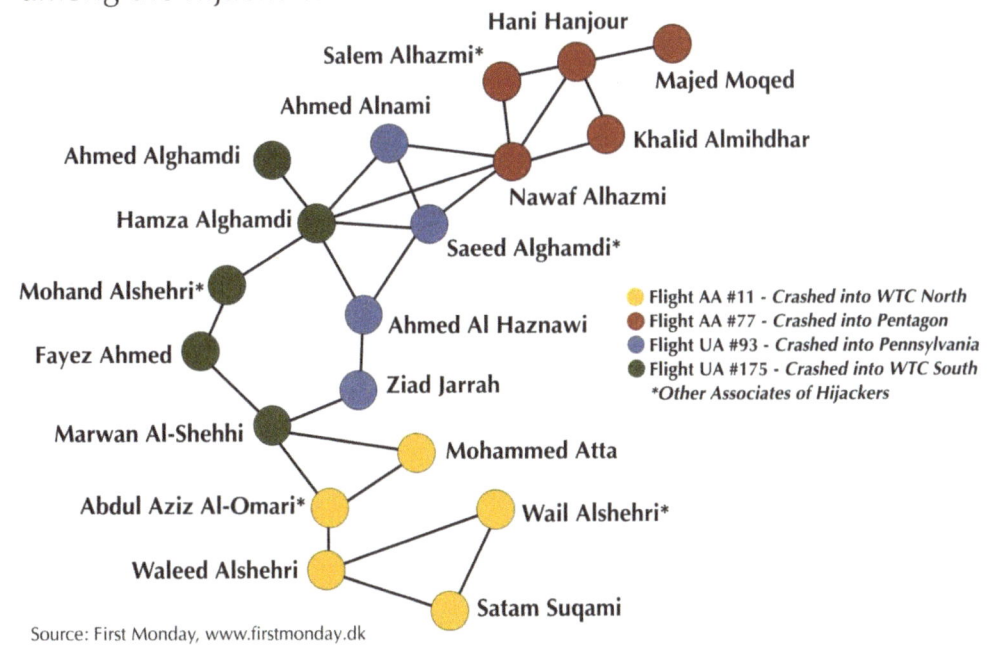

Source: First Monday, www.firstmonday.dk

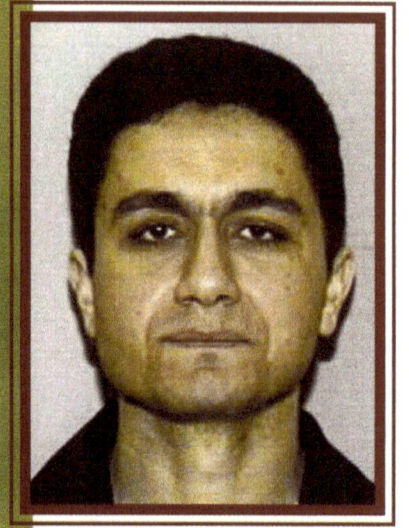

Mohammed Atta, the hijacker who piloted the plane that crashed into the north tower of the World Trade Center, often visited Nawaf Alhazmi and Khalid Almihdhar.

In the middle of January, Alhazmi and Almihdhar flew from Bangkok, Thailand, to Los Angeles. They stayed with Hanjour in San Diego. Mohammed Atta, the pilot of the plane that crashed into the north tower of the World Trade Center on September 11, 2001, often visited them.

In May 2001, Alhazmi and Almihdhar took three weeks of flight training lessons at Sorbi's Flying Club in San Diego. They told the instructor that they wanted to fly Boeings, but they were restricted to a twin-engine Cessna. The men were not quick studies.

Alhazmi and Almihdhar entered the United States again on business visas in July 2001. They gave a Marriott hotel in New York City as their address. In August, the FBI put the two men on a watch list.

The Final Plans

Hanjour kept trying to improve his piloting skills. In June 2001, Al Qaeda sent an Algerian pilot, Lotfi Raissi, to the United States to help Hanjour train on a jet simulator. The practice may not have been a lot of help. In August 2001, Hanjour flew three times with instructors at a flight school in Bowie, Maryland, outside of Washington, D.C. Once again, his instructors weren't impressed with his ability. They refused to let him rent a plane.

Nawaf Alhazmi and Khalid Almihdhar went to Las Vegas in August 2001, where they met with the four pilots who would fly the hijacked planes on September 11. The six men stayed in cheap hotels. They probably worked on details of the planned attacks. This followed the Al Qaeda pattern of keeping cells separate. The cell members come together only shortly before an attack. Ordinarily, cell members have face-to-face meetings in secure rooms, and instructions are often given in a coded language.

By September of 2001, Hani Hanjour, Nawaf Alhazmi, Khalid Almihdhar, thirty-year-old Salem Alhazmi, and another Saudi, twenty-four-year-old Majed Moqed, were sharing a $280-a-week room at the Valencia Motel in Laurel, Maryland, a suburb of Washington, D.C. According to neighbors, the men drove a blue Toyota and always went out together. They paid regular visits to Gold's Gym in Greenbelt, Maryland.

Deadly Preparations

A document found in Nawaf Alhazmi's car titled "The Last Night" gives a glimpse of what went through the minds of the five men on September 10. The document instructs them "to pledge of allegiance for death and renewal of intent." It tells

This display was set up outside of the Pentagon crash site and featured the names and brief biographies of all the victims of the attack, including Charles Frank Burlingame III, the pilot of American Airlines Flight 77.

them to read and understand certain chapters in the Koran. Many times they are urged to pray to Allah and to cleanse their hearts. There is advice on how to fight and the instruction to take a shower. One of the passages that must have inspired them reads, "Smile in the face of death, oh young man! For you are on your way to the everlasting paradise!"

The Passengers

On the morning of September 11, 2001, the five men arrived at Dulles Airport in Virginia, where they boarded American Airlines Flight 77 bound for Los Angeles. In their car they left

Preparations

a cashier's check made out to a flight school in Phoenix, a box-cutter knife, drawings of the cockpit of a Boeing 757, and a map of Washington, D.C.

Fifty-three other passengers boarded Flight 77. Among them were two staff members of the National Geographic Society, three teachers, and three students. The eight were headed to California. The three students, eleven-year-old sixth graders, had been selected to be part of a program at the Channel Islands National Marine Sanctuary near Santa Barbara, California. The program, a Sustainable Seas Expedition, lets the students work with biologists to monitor ocean life and activity. The kids had also planned to kayak and hike to various study areas. The students were from middle schools in Washington, D.C., and were excited to be going on this adventure. An adult who went to the airport with them said that the kids wore their National Geographic caps and marched past the check-in counter as if to say, "We're on official business."

The pilot, Charles Burlingame, who had landed wounded F-4 Phantoms on the deck of an aircraft carrier in high seas, sat at the controls. At about 8:00 AM Eastern Standard Time, Flight 77 taxied out to the runway. It was a beautiful spring day in Washington.

Washington Dulles International Airport terminal *(above)* and ticket counters *(below)*

THE ATTACK

CHAPTER

At 8:19 AM on September 11, 2001, the control tower at Dulles Airport informed Flight 77 that it was cleared for takeoff. Flight 77 left the ground, heading west across northern Virginia and West Virginia. The tower instructed the pilot to climb to 11,000 feet. For the next few minutes the pilot and tower stayed in contact as Flight 77 avoided other incoming and outgoing planes. The plane climbed to 33,000 feet and continued west. About twenty minutes into the flight, the control tower in Indianapolis took over from the Washington air route traffic control.

The Attack on the Pentagon on September 11, 2001

Flight 77 Disappears

At 8:56 AM Flight 77 neared the Ohio-Kentucky border. The Indianapolis control tower tried to contact the pilot. After two minutes with no response, the controller called the American Airlines dispatcher. The dispatcher tried unsuccessfully to contact the plane.

The control tower had not only lost radio contact, the plane had disappeared from the radar screens. The tower alerted other control sectors to watch for the plane. At 9:09 AM word came that United Airlines Flight 175 had hit the World Trade Center. Suspicion must have started growing. Like Flight 77, that plane had been headed for Los Angeles.

Aboard Flight 77, the terror had started. Passengers making frantic calls to loved ones from their cell phones reported that several men with knives and box cutters had overpowered the crew and taken over the cockpit. The hijackers pushed the passengers and crew to the back of the plane. The hijackers turned off the transponder, the device that sends information to the control tower's radar screens. Investigators later said that action proved the hijackers had knowledge of flying a plane. The hijacker pilot, probably Hani Hanjour, turned the plane east, back toward Washington. As the plane neared the city, it flew low over the Columbia Pike, one of the main roads that leads to the Pentagon.

(right) Ed Flynn, the Arlington, Virginia, police chief, presents Sheri Burlingame with a special "CPT 77" license plate in honor of her husband, Charles, the pilot of Flight 77.

(left) Rescue workers pause for a break at the Pentagon crash site.

(right) H. G. Whittington holds a picture of his daughter Leslie and granddaughter Zoe, who died in the crash of Flight 77.

The Attack on the Pentagon on September 11, 2001

Flight 77 Reappears

Shortly after 9:30 AM controllers at Dulles Airport saw an unidentified aircraft headed at high speed toward the restricted airspace around the White House. Controllers hurriedly called Reagan National Airport in Washington and the White House to warn them of the possible attack.

Flight 77 neared the Pentagon. The hijacker-pilot made a difficult high-speed turn as he descended. The plane dropped 7,000 feet in two minutes. At 9:38 AM the pilot of Flight 77 throttled up the engines and slammed the plane into the Pentagon at 460 miles an hour. The impact took a 30-yard by 10-yard slice out of the building and sent a fireball 60 feet into the air. The massive building shook.

A man walking near the building as the aircraft approached heard a terrible noise. As he looked around, he saw the plane clip a couple of light poles on the way in. He fell flat, convinced that if he didn't the plane would hit him.

The Reaction

Secretary of Defense Donald Rumsfeld ran from his office on the opposite side of the building to the attack site. He helped put some of the injured onto stretchers. Then he went to the National Military Command Center (NMCC), located in the lower floors of the Pentagon.

From the NMCC the leaders in the Pentagon can observe and control actions by the Department of Defense

The Attack

anywhere in the world. The NMCC staff constantly monitors conditions worldwide, particularly concerning nuclear command and control, and missile warning systems. Despite the smoke that seeped into the room, the staff remained in the

> **WHEN FLIGHT 77 HIT THE PENTAGON:**
>
> - It penetrated twenty-four-inch-thick walls—six inches of limestone, eight inches of brick, and ten inches of concrete.
> - It went through five-inch concrete floors.
> - It made a hole 100 feet wide.
> - It damaged three of the five rings.
> - It killed 189 people.

center. The Pentagon placed the military on Threatcom Delta—the highest alert status short of war.

Upstairs, Pentagon workers helped each other out of their offices and the building. Some people had to run across the burning airplane to get out. Rescue workers and employees fought their way through black smoke and heat. Throughout the Pentagon voices could be heard calling out to anyone who might still be inside. Those in the undamaged parts of the building took the time to secure classified items before leaving.

The Arlington County police and fire departments arrived and pumped water on the fire. Medical professionals driving by set up triage areas in the parking lot. Many passersby transported the injured to hospitals in their private vehicles. Helicopters flew the most seriously wounded to

Firefighters struggle to put out the flames at the Pentagon on September 11, 2001, while onlookers watch from a distance.

area hospitals. The official forces were bolstered by search and rescue experts, FBI agents, and Federal Emergency Management Agency (FEMA) teams.

At 10:10 AM the part of the Pentagon next to the impact area collapsed. After the collapse, firefighters and rescue workers had to wait to go back in until the portion could be stabilized.

By this time, much of Washington had been evacuated. This included the White House, the Capitol, all federal office buildings, the Supreme Court, and all the museums and monuments. Foreign embassies shut down, as well as international financial organizations. The exodus led to massive gridlock on the roads.

On September 13, 2001, firefighters were still trying to put out "hot spots" where the fire from the September 11 crash continued to smoulder and flare up.

The Federal Aviation Administration (FAA) ordered all commercial and private aircraft flying in the United States to land at the nearest airport. By 10:30 AM F-16 and F-15 fighter planes patrolled the skies over Washington in response to reports that more hijacked planes were on the way. By the end of the day, some of the fighters had been in the air for over eight hours. Early in the afternoon, five warships and two aircraft carriers left the U.S. Naval Station in Norfolk, Virginia. Their mission was to protect the East Coast and to reduce the number of ships in the port.

A small crisis occurred when the cell phone network around the Pentagon overloaded. Those who could get through passed along phone numbers and messages. The fire at the building proved to be a tough problem. Materials in the roof burned and were almost impossible to get at. Pools of jet fuel ignited. At 9:30 PM the fire was still not under control.

Structural Pluses

One small piece of good news was that the area of the Pentagon that Flight 77 struck had been undergoing remodeling and was not yet fully occupied. In addition, some of the renovations may have allowed more people to escape. Vertical steel beams had been placed on either side of every window, and a strong mesh material, similar to the Kevlar used in bulletproof vests, had been stretched between the steel beams to catch debris in the event of an explosion. The windows themselves had been replaced with inch-and-a-half-thick panes of blast-resistant glass.

Two employees of the contractor for the renovation had been on the fifth floor of the outermost ring, about 75 feet from the point of impact. The area immediately filled with black smoke. The two crawled on their hands and knees

Evacuated Pentagon military personnel walk down nearby highway I-395 toward safety on September 11, 2001.

On September 11, 2001, a rescue helicopter uses Washington Boulevard outside the Pentagon to land and pick up injured personnel evacuated from the building.

checking every office on the fifth floor to make sure that everyone got out. They then went down to the fourth, third, and second floors, where they again checked the offices. The contractor believed that renovations kept the structure from collapsing for a half hour. They also slowed the plane as it entered the building.

On the evening of September 11, Secretary Rumsfeld held a press conference in the Pentagon as the fire continued to burn. He said, "The Pentagon is functioning. It will be in business tomorrow."

Damage to the west face of the Pentagon after the September 11 attack

THE CLEANUP AND INVESTIGATION

CHAPTER 5

Efforts to find survivors and remove bodies continued around the clock at the Pentagon. The process was often slowed by the necessity to shore up the collapsed portion of the building. The final death toll was 189—64 (including passengers, crewmembers, and hijackers) on the airplane and 125 people in the Pentagon.

Most of the fuselage of the plane stayed intact after the impact. Searchers hunting through the rubble heard signals from the plane's black box. They found the box on the Friday after the attack. Both the recorders inside had been damaged. The recorders

The Attack on the Pentagon on September 11, 2001

AN AIRPLANE'S BLACK BOX

The black box (which is actually orange to aid searchers) is mounted in the tail of the plane. It is made of insulated titanium to protect it from fire, impact, and water pressure. Two recorders inside the box collect over 300 pieces of information.

Cockpit data recorder tapes:	flight crew conversations cockpit sounds engine noises
Flight data recorder tapes (partial list):	time wing angle latitude and longitude wing flap position airspeed landing gear position altitude air pressure heading temperature thrust wind shear

were sent to a laboratory at the National Transportation Safety Board in Washington. Unfortunately, the technicians were not able to get any useful information from them.

FEMA Search and Rescue

FEMA flew in several urban search and rescue (US&R) teams to help with the recovery. These teams coordinate the local emergency personnel into a unified force. They brief local officials on public assistance and make plans for removing the debris. To be certified by FEMA, US&R teams must meet several criteria. The members are all certified emergency medical technicians. They can be deployed in six hours.

The Cleanup and Investigation

They can sustain themselves (provide food, shelter, etc.) for seventy-two hours. Each group has sixty-two members who can fill thirty-one positions, including engineers, search specialists with trained dogs, physicians, nurses, hazardous materials specialists, and communications personnel.

Once the teams got to the Pentagon, they set up a base of operations. The search specialists checked blueprints and then went into the damaged area. As they went they braced areas that were in danger of collapsing. Then searchers with dogs went inside.

US&R teams stay on a site until it is determined that no more victims will be found alive. The last team left the Pentagon on September 22, 2001.

The FBI Investigation

Two weeks after the attack, the FBI took control of the Pentagon site. That turned the investigation into a criminal one. As the crews went into the wreckage they examined the rubble. The loads of debris were taken to a parking lot. Crime-scene technicians cataloged potential evidence. In the first two weeks workers removed over 10,000 tons of debris. Fifteen hundred people worked on the cleanup and investigation. The FBI estimated that they would be at the scene for a month going through the debris.

Three months after the attack, the U.S. Army had a more delicate task to perform. Thousands of people had left mementos on a hill overlooking the Pentagon. Wreaths,

Rescuers and investigators used construction equipment to remove debris from the damaged areas of the Pentagon.

flowers, photographs, notes, teddy bears, and flags covered the ground. To protect the offerings from the weather, the army decided to store them for safekeeping and later display some in a permanent memorial. The movers took their time packing the mementos that expressed the condolences of strangers and the unity that Americans showed after the attacks.

As the cleanup efforts continued, the FBI quickly identified the hijackers. Sixteen of the nineteen men on all four planes had definite ties to Osama bin Laden. All of the pilots had been trained in the United States. More than 7,000 federal investigators worked on the investigation. They entered data including phone bills, ATM receipts, fake IDs, and Islamic verse into computers. They hoped to find patterns that connected the hijackers with others who might have been involved in the attacks.

In the days following September 11, families of the Pentagon victims constructed a memorial near the crash site with flowers, flags, and notes.

Other Suspects

Several men with suspected ties to the hijackers were questioned and detained. Osama Awadallah was arrested in San Diego after FBI agents found his name and phone number in Nawaf Alhazmi's car. Lotfi Raissi, the man who had supposedly given jet simulator lessons to Hani Hanjour, was arrested in London. A third man, Faisal Michael Al Salmi, was accused of lying to the FBI about his ties to Hanjour. He was transported from Arizona to New York for questioning.

On December 11, 2001, the Department of Justice brought the first indictment against a terrorist allegedly involved in the September 11 attacks. A grand jury in Virginia charged Zacarias Moussaoui, a French-born Moroccan, with conspiring with Al Qaeda and Osama bin Laden to kill thousands of innocent people on September 11. The indictment against him places him at a terrorist camp in

The Attack on the Pentagon on September 11, 2001

Afghanistan in 1998. Officials believe that Moussaoui was supposed to be the twentieth hijacker.

Moussaoui came to the United States in February 2001 wanting to learn to fly. After he failed out of a flight school in Oklahoma, he went to a flight school in Minnesota, where he paid $6,300 in cash to use flight simulators. The instructors became suspicious of the cash payments and contacted the FBI. Moussaoui was detained on August 17 for immigration violations. He has been in jail ever since.

Some of the evidence the FBI found in Moussaoui's possession were flight manuals for the Boeing 747, a flight-simulator computer program, two knives, fighting shields, and a laptop computer. Moussaoui also had the phone number of Ramzi bin al-Shibh, a member of the Hamburg, Germany, Al Qaeda cell, who had sent money to Moussaoui. Al-Shibh had twice been denied a visa to travel to the United States.

The charges against Moussaoui ran to thirty pages, much of it showing how his actions paralleled those of the hijackers. The indictment lists six counts of conspiracy against Moussaoui: conspiracies to commit terrorism, to commit aircraft piracy, to destroy aircraft, to use weapons of mass destruction, to murder United States employees, and to destroy property. The first four charges carry the death penalty; the last two have a life sentence.

As Moussaoui awaits his trial he is confined to his cell in a maximum security prison for twenty-two hours a day

The Cleanup and Investigation

An artist's rendering of Zacarias Moussaoui as he appeared at an arraignment on January 2, 2002. He was charged with conspiring with other Al Qaeda members in the September 11 attacks.

without radio, television, videos, or music. On March 28, 2002, U.S. Attorney General John Ashcroft announced that he would seek the death penalty if Moussaoui is convicted of the charges against him. Ashcroft told the public that his reason for seeking the death penalty was "the impact of the crime on thousands of victims." He continued, "To that end, we remain committed not only to carrying out justice . . . but also to ensuring that the rights of the victims are fully protected."

Pentagon Renovation Program manager Walker Lee Evey describes the damage caused by the crash of Flight 77 into the Pentagon.

THE AFTERMATH

CHAPTER 6

Flight 77 crashed into Wedge 1 of the Pentagon, the part that had just undergone a complete renovation. Some of the employees had returned to their offices in the renovated area. The area was days away from completion. The workers who had spent almost four years to renovate the section saw their efforts destroyed in a matter of seconds.

The Renovation

The renovation of the Pentagon began in 1998. The Pentagon had not had a major overhaul in its fifty-eight years, and the need was urgent. Much had changed since 1941. At the time the Pentagon was

The Attack on the Pentagon on September 11, 2001

built, there was one telephone for every three employees. By 1998, each person had two computers, one classified and one not classified, and a telephone. New wires had simply been laid on top of old ones. They ran above the ceiling panels, through floor conduits, and along hallways. In addition, the building did not meet current health and fire codes. It was not in total compliance with the Americans with Disabilities Act.

The building had been constructed in five parts, or wedges, connected to one another by expansion joints. The original plan was to work on one 1,000,000-square-foot wedge at a time. When the renovation started, all of the personnel who worked in Wedge 1 were moved into other offices in the Pentagon or into leased space. The contractors then took out everything down to the concrete slabs and columns. They removed twenty-eight million pounds of asbestos-contaminated material.

Life-Saving Features

Some of the innovations that kept the number of September 11 casualties down were steel beams that went through all five floors, replacing the concrete columns. Kevlar cloth between the beams kept debris from flying. The specially treated blast-proof glass windows stayed mostly intact even after the crash. They should have, as each window weighs 1,500 pounds and costs $10,000.

Other changes were designed to make the building safer and more efficient. Alterations to the ventilation system

Secretary of Defense Donald Rumsfeld *(left)* is updated on the status of the Pentagon reconstruction by project manager Walker Lee Evey on the six-month anniversary of the September 11 attacks.

guard against nuclear, chemical, and biological attacks. The sprinkler system will be updated. Safety measures include putting glow-in-the-dark devices at floor level. The thinking behind this is that, in case of a fire, a person would be crawling and would not be looking for exit signs overhead.

The Pentagon was declared a historic structure in 1992, so the contractor was required to rebuild it to its original form. To replace the outside face, the contractor went back to the limestone quarry in Indiana where the original stone was quarried sixty years ago in order to match the original stone.

When engineers inspected the damaged part of the Pentagon, they found small fractures in many of the columns. These were probably a result of the intense heat from the fire.

The Attack on the Pentagon on September 11, 2001

The most severe damage was confined to Wedges 1 and 2. The contractor immediately began demolishing the damaged parts and got ready to restore Wedge 1—again.

The Rebuilding Team

The devastating attack inspired the workers. They named the rebuilding the Phoenix Project, after the mythological bird that rose from ashes. Demolition of the damaged section was completed in just two months, removing 10,000 tons of debris. The renovation is proceeding from the outside to the inside. Will Colsten, the manager of the project, told *McGraw-Hill Construction* that this is not the most efficient way to do the work. However, from a national sense of pride "it is more important to have the outside finished first." By January 2002, more than 1,000 employees had returned to their new offices.

Over 600 people worked on the rebuilding. They worked in two ten-hour shifts a day, six days a week. Some workers protested when they were told they had to take two days off at Christmas. A digital clock counted down the seconds to the projected completion day, September 11, 2002. In the early 1940s, the Pentagon cost nearly $50 million to build. The total cost now, including the rebuilding of the damaged area, will be $3 billion.

War Against Terrorism

In the first six months after the attacks, intelligence agencies foiled a number of terrorist attacks. These included attacks in

The Aftermath

Singapore and on American embassies in other parts of the world. In an interview with cable networks, Secretary of Defense Donald Rumsfeld said, "Our effort is worldwide, and it involves all elements of national power. It involves shutting down bank accounts, arresting people, law enforcement, maritime intercept of ships as a deterrent to see that they don't transfer terrorists or terrorist capabilities."

United States intelligence agencies captured and questioned several members of the Al Qaeda network, including Abu Zubaydah, the network operations chief. Osama bin Laden and Taliban leader Mullah Omar remain at large.

PENTAGON MEMORIAL

The Bybee Stone Company in Elletsville, Indiana, has created a memorial stone for the Pentagon crash site. The stone carries the words of President George W. Bush: "Terrorist attacks can shake the foundations of our biggest buildings, but they cannot touch the foundation of America." The stone was signed by the quarry workers at Bybee, and by some of the hundreds of construction workers who worked on the project.

On the nine-month anniversary of the attacks, officials dedicated a piece of the original Pentagon facade, along with mementos of the attack, as part of a "dedication capsule."

The war in Afghanistan drove the Taliban from power in Afghanistan and disrupted, but didn't eliminate the Al Qaeda organization. U.S. forces are tracking terrorist groups in the Philippines, Somalia, Yemen, northern Iraq, and Georgia in southeast Europe. Three hundred suspected Al Qaeda and Taliban fighters are being held for questioning at the U.S. Naval Base in Guantanamo Bay, Cuba.

At a Pentagon ceremony on September 11, 2002, Donald Rumsfeld applauded the construction crews, saying, "In a sense, we meet on a battlefield. If it does not appear so today, that is because of the singular devotion of the men and women who worked day and night to fulfill a solemn vow that not one stone of this building be out of place on this anniversary."

The attacks on the United States on September 11, 2001, were devastating and horrible. Through it all, the American people stood firm. They grieved and then set about the task of rebuilding and ridding the world of terrorism. Like the massive Pentagon, they were bent but not broken.

GLOSSARY

Allah The word by which Muslims refer to the divine being.

appropriate To set something aside for a particular purpose. This term often refers to a governmental body deciding how taxpayer money will be spent.

classified Refers to sensitive items, such as papers and tape recordings, that can be shown only to certain people because of national security concerns.

condolences Expressions of sympathy to others.

deploy To place forces where they will be best able to do their job. This often refers to military troops.

exodus A large number of people leaving a certain place.

extremist A person who advocates radical religious or political measures.

fatwa An Islamic religious decree.

indictment The legal process by which a person is accused of a crime.

infidel A person who rejects the faith of a particular religion.

jihad A holy war fought on behalf of Islam, or any crusade or struggle.

militant Aggressive and ready to fight.

FOR MORE INFORMATION

Federal Bureau of Investigation
Department of Justice
935 Pennsylvania Avenue NW
Washington, DC 20535
(202) 324-3000
Web site: http://www.fbi.gov

Federal Emergency Management Agency
500 C Street SW
Washington, DC 20472
(202) 566-1600
Web site: http://www.fema.gov

U.S. Department of Defense
Office of the Secretary of Defense
1400 Defense Pentagon, Room 3A750
Washington, DC 20301-1400
(703) 428-0711
Web site: http://www.defenselink.mil

For More Information

U.S. Department of Justice
950 Pennsylvania Avenue NW
Washington, DC 20530-0001
(202) 353-1555
Web site: http://www.usdoj.gov

U.S. Department of State
2201 C Street NW
Washington, DC 20520
(202) 647-4000
Web site: http://www.state.gov

Video

Modern Marvels: The Pentagon. 2001. Part of a series broadcast by the History Channel.

Web Sites

Due to the changing nature of Internet links, the Rosen Publishing Group, Inc., has developed an online list of Web sites related to the subject of this book. This site is updated regularly. Please use this link to access the list:

http://www.rosenlinks.com/ta/atpe

For Further Reading

Alexander, Yonah, and Michael Swetnam. *Usama bin Laden's al-Qaida: Profile of a Terrorist Network.* Ardsley, NY: Transnational Publishers, Inc., 2001.

America's Heroes: Inspiring Stories of Courage, Sacrifice and Patriotism. Champaign, IL: Peter L. Bannon, 2001.

Gaines, Ann G. *Terrorism.* Philadelphia: Chelsea House Publishers, 1999.

Goldberg, Alfred. *The Pentagon: The First Fifty Years.* Washington, DC: U.S. Government Printing Office, 1992.

Landau, Ellen. *Osama bin Laden: A War Against the West.* Brookfield, CT: Twenty-First Century Books, 2002.

Reeve, Simon. *The New Jackals.* Boston: Northeastern University Press, 1999.

Shingle, Barbara. *Day of Terror: September 11, 2001.* Beaverton, OR: American Products Publishing Co., 2001.

BIBLIOGRAPHY

ABC News. "Who Did It?" January 9, 2002. Retrieved March 2002 (http://abcnews.go.com/sections/us/DailyNews/WTC_suspects.html).

Attorney General Transcript, News Conference—DOJ to Seek Death Penalty Against Moussaoui, March 28, 2002.

Attorney General Transcript, News Conference regarding Zacarias Moussaoui, December 11, 2001.

Caruso, J. T., before the Subcommittee on International Operations and Terrorism, Committee of Foreign Relations. United States Senate. December 18, 2001.

CBS News. "Primary Target." Retrieved April 2002 (http://www.cbsnews.com/stories/2001/09/11/national/main/31072.shtml).

CBS News. "Translated Text: Hijackers' How-To." Retrieved April 2002 (http://www.cbsnews.com/stories/2001/10/01/archive/main313163.shtml).

Downey, Sarah. "Who Is Zacarias Moussaoui?" *Newsweek*, December 14, 2001.

The Attack on the Pentagon on September 11, 2001

"Fact Sheet: Terrorism." Federal Emergency Management Agency. September 23, 2001. Retrieved April 2002 (www.fema.gov/library/terror.htm).

Frontline. "Al Qaeda." 2001. Retrieved April 2002 (http://www.pbs.org/wgbh/pages/frontline/shows/binladen/who/alqaeda.html).

Mader, Robert P. "Tougher Pentagon to Rise." *Contractor*, July 2001.

"National Military Command Center." Federation of American Scientists. Retrieved March 2002 (http://www.fas.org/nuke/guide/usa/c3i/nmcc.htm).

Online NewsHour, PBS. "Flight Data and Voice Recorders Found at Pentagon." Retrieved March 2002 (http://www.pbs.org/newsupdates/september01/wash_9-14.html).

Tanner, Victoria L. "Pentagon Gets Back to Business." Construction.com. Retrieved March 2002 (http://www.designbuildmag.com/dec2001/pentagon1201.asp).

Thomas, Evan. "Cracking the Terror Code." *Newsweek*, October 15, 2001.

U.S. Department of State. "The Hijackings." Retrieved March 2002 (http://usinfo.state.gov/products/pubs/terrornet/print/sbhijack.htm).

INDEX

A
Afghanistan, 15, 16, 17, 19, 20, 22, 48, 56
Al Qaeda, 15, 16–18, 55, 56
    September 11 hijackers and, 25–29, 46, 47–48
    structure of, 20–22
    terrorism and, 18, 20, 22–23
    training camps, 18, 20, 47
Atta, Mohammed, 28

B
bin Laden, Osama, 15–19, 20, 22, 27, 55
    in Sudan, 17, 18, 19
    ties to September 11 hijackers, 46, 47
black boxes, 43–44
Burlingame, Charles, 31

D
Dulles Airport, 33, 36

F
Federal Bureau of Investigation (FBI), 18–19, 20, 28, 38
    investigation of Pentagon attack, 45, 46–47, 48
Federal Emergency Management Agency (FEMA), 38, 44–45
Flight 77, American Airlines, 30, 33–36, 40, 43, 51
    passengers of, 31, 43

H
hijackers of September 11 terrorist attacks, 20–21, 23, 31, 34
    identification of, 46
    other suspects, 47–49
    planning attacks, 25–30

M
Moqed, Majed, 29
Moussaoui, Zacarias, 47–49

P
Pentagon
    building of, 5, 9–12, 52–53
    design of, 11–12
    need for, 7–8, 13
    rebuilding of (post–Sept. 11), 5, 54
    renovation of (pre–Sept. 11), 51–54
Pentagon, attack on (September 11, 2001), 4, 13, 33–41
    aftermath of, 36–40, 43–46
    FBI investigation into, 45, 46–47
    memorial for, 55
    rescue/recovery efforts, 37–38, 40–41, 43, 44–45
    victims of, 37, 43

R
Rumsfeld, Donald, 36, 41, 55, 56

T
Taliban, the 19, 55, 56
terrorism, war against, 54–56

U
U.S. Department of Defense, 36
USS *Cole* attack, 22, 27
U.S. War Department, 7, 8

W
World Trade Center
    1993 bombing of, 18–19
    September 11, 2001, attack, 28, 34
World War II, 7–8, 12, 13

The Attack on the Pentagon on September 11, 2001

About the Author
Carolyn Gard writes from her home in Boulder, Colorado. She divides her time between writing, doing research for the Colorado state legislature, and hiking with her three German shepherd dogs.

Photo Credits
Cover, pp. 5, 10, 17, 19, 23, 24–25, 26, 28, 35 (top, second from bottom, bottom), 42–43, 46, 47, 49, 53, 55, 56 © AP/Wide World Photos; pp. 6–7 © TimePix; p. 12 © Bettmann/Corbis; pp. 14–15, 30, 38, 41 © Reuters NewMedia Inc./Corbis; pp. 16, 32–33 (bottom), 35 (second from top), 39, 40, 50–51 © AFP/Corbis; p. 27 courtesy of http://www.firstmonday.dk; pp. 32–33 © Angelo Homak/Corbis.

Editor
Christine Poolos

Series Design and Layout
Geri Giordano

www.ingramcontent.com/pod-product-compliance
Lightning Source LLC
Chambersburg PA
CBHW041115070526
44584CB00002B/173